# KEEP WALKING

*How to get from A to C, when stuck at B.*

## MAVELA OWUSU BOAHEN

ISBN: 978-1-5272-2011-9

*Book Cover Design:*
Michael Boadi (**mbn**limited)
mbnstudioz@yahoo/gmail.com

*Interior Book Design:*
Mavis Osei-Boakye (Print Discoveries Ltd.)
printdiscoveries@gmail.com

*Editor:*
Alison Parkin

# *Foreward*

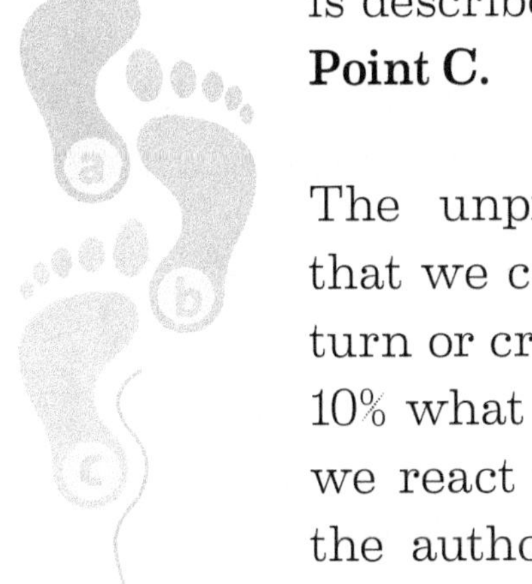

Life is a journey and it takes more than daily existence to make it fulfilling. Some people throw in the towel and accept defeat when things don't go in their favour, others surrender and go with the flow not looking forward to anything different in their daily life. A few have chosen to take appropriate steps to redeem lost time by reflecting over their shortcomings and picking up the 'left-overs' to make a fresh start in order to achieve their dream which is described by Mavela in this book as **Point C.**

The unpredictability of life means that we can never anticipate the next turn or crossroads. Life, we are told, is 10% what happens to us and 90% how we react to it. Such is the spirit that the author of this book depicts, and hopefully serves to inspire readers who may find themselves at **Point A** to take the appropriate steps towards **Point C**; but, if they are broken down at **Point B**, they must not make it a destination point but press on to **Point C.**

Usually the decisions we take when going through transitions in our lives have huge importance on the general outcomes of our actions. From teenage to young adult life, student to real life, single to married, childless to parenthood, jobless to employee, all are forms of transitions we will face one way or the other. But the 'in-between-decisions', melt-downs and challenges require skill, wisdom, mentoring, coaching and guidance in order to make it through any transition (**Point B).**

In '**KEEP WALKING - How to get from A to C, when stuck at B**', Mavela Owusu Boahen has gracefully shared her life journey with readers and the details will inspire them to keep walking if not running.

*Well done Mavela!*
*Grant Bulmuo*
*Speaker, Author & Lead Consultant*
*of Neogenics Education Group*

# Acknowledgements

I would like to start off by firstly thanking the Creator.

Secondly, I would like to thank my parents, my husband, Joe and son Sebastian.

Thirdly, I would like to thank Twishika, who was my main inspiration for this book, I hope, like other readers of this book, you will be inspired to keep walking.

Lastly, I would like to thank you for reading this book. Having done this you have helped to make my dreams a reality.

*Mavela*

# CONTENTS

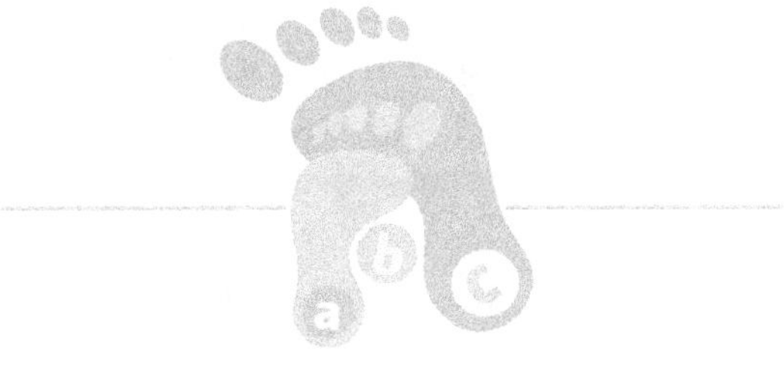



# CHAPTER ONE

# Introduction

Hi, my name is Mavela Owusu Boahen, previously Mavela Daley. I am a wife, mother and, by profession, a teacher. However, a few years ago this was not the case. Becoming a primary school teacher was my chosen career goal, the destination I refer to as 'C' throughout this book.

However, somewhere along the way, I found myself at a place that was despairingly miles away from that goal, the place I refer to as 'B' in the book. The circumstances that caused me to arrive at B left me feeling utter despair and hopelessness.

Others might have accepted what they believed to be their fate and remained at B, finding it easier to accept the status quo and settle into a comfort zone. Regardless, I chose to believe in myself: my dreams, goals, gifts, skills, experience and potential. I chose to keep my vision alive! I arrived at B in 2010 but, the following year, I made a drastic decision which would enable me to continue to C. That decision involved quitting a job that I had been doing for just 8 months. Consequently, by 2014, I found myself just a few miles away from C.

## *By July 2015, I had arrived!*

In this book, you will discover how I consciously and deliberately raised myself from the rock bottom of B, where I had found myself, and understand the steps that I took to help me to arrive at C.

Have no doubt, there were obstacles along the way and at times my arrival at C seemed impossible. Nevertheless, through much perseverance and by keeping my vision alive, I was able to overcome those obstacles to finally reach my goal.

In writing this book, my desire is to inspire you to continue to pursue your goals and dreams, despite what has happened in your life - whatever you think has derailed you and led you to reach and remain beached at B. I also hope that, through reading this book, you will be motivated to take the actions which will lead you closer to your 'C'.

Ultimately, my heartfelt desire for you is that, through much prayer, hope, dedication and hard work, you will arrive at your own C.

*Happy Reading!*

*Mavela.*

# Before England

The place I refer to as 'A' in this book represents the very commencement of my life. I was born in 1988 on the small Caribbean island of Montserrat. My mother already had a child when she met and married my father so, although I was her second child, I was my father's first.

From memory and by my own analysis, my life started off quite well. I clearly remember the warmth and security of being reared in a two parent household and the laughter and joy I shared with my siblings.

I recall being enthusiastic about reading, learning and dance. More importantly, I also remember excelling at school, receiving 90% or above in my exams. Generally, life had started off well for me. That was until 1995.

In July 1995, Montserrat's volcano awoke violently from its sleep, disrupting our lives for good. My family and I had to leave our warm home in the East and relocate to the unfamiliar North. The journey from our home to the North was treacherous and we were sorely afraid. I remember riding in the back of my parents' car with my three younger siblings and my older half-sister, feeling very afraid, not really understanding what had happened, why it was happening to us and what would be the consequences. The usually clear blue sky was grey and the alien ash beat violently down on our little red car as we journeyed to safety. My small heart palpitated listening to the raucous sound of thunder and glimpsing flashes of lighting.

For a short while, we had to live in a derelict school building before moving to live with an aunt. I vaguely remember feeling out of place in that derelict building, not having a cosy bed of my own, or a place to have a quiet, warm shower. Our living space was shared with others, as were our rationed meals.

When we arrived to stay with our aunt, we found the living conditions were much better, cosy beds, kindly relations and rich home-cooked meals. However, it was still not our home and I sort of sensed that things would never be the same again.

As the situation in Montserrat worsened, we had no choice but to sadly leave our little green paradise in the Caribbean Sea and relocate to England.

## England

Upon arriving in England in September 1997, we lived temporarily with an uncle, who had lived here for many years, before finally moving to a flat in Hackney. This became our permanent home. At that moment in time, my family numbered seven - my mum, dad, my older half-sister (14), my younger sister (7), my twin siblings (3) and myself (8).

So, at the age of eight, I started my new life in England. It was all very new:  the weather, the transport system, the people, the accents, the culture but I was soon to get used to it.

Another thing that would be new to me, was the education system. This would be an important area in my life as it was the vehicle that enabled me to arrive at C.

## Northwold Primary School

In 1998, at the age of 8, I began my primary school education in England in Year 4 at Northwold Primary, a welcoming and nurturing school. I enjoyed studying at this school and did not feel different or out of place, but felt just as important as all the other pupils who, unlike myself, had not just relocated from another country. I made friends quite quickly although I did experience a small degree of bullying. Nonetheless, my thirst for knowledge and education continued. I enjoyed learning and becoming completely and wholehearted involved in a range of activities. By the end of my two years at primary school, my skills and passion for learning had not diminished at all, in fact I had rather excelled. I left primary school with two level 5s (strong passes) and one level 4 (a good pass) in the SATS -Standard Attainment Tests.

## *Haggerston Girls' Secondary School*

The grades that I had achieved at primary school ensured that I had a great academic start to secondary school. Like primary school, it was a new experience but by this time I was more familiar with the culture and lifestyle and the academic system. I also had a British accent by then! For the most part, I was extremely focused at secondary school. I believe this was largely due to my strict Christian upbringing coupled with my love for learning and access to very good teachers.

I think this was the formula for my success and, by 2005, I had achieved ten GCSEs: 3 A*s and 7 As.

It was around this time that, naturally, I started to think about the career that I wanted to pursue. I decided that I wanted to become an Educational Psychologist. I did some research and found out that, as well as the actual qualifications, to become an Educational Psychologist, one needed to possess a few years of teaching experience as well. This became my career plan.

## *LaSwap Sixth Form*

With the grades that I had achieved at GCSE level and the long-term career goal of becoming an Educational Psychologist in mind, I was naturally advised to apply to study A levels. My secondary school teachers encouraged me to select a "prestigious" sixth form to study subjects at A level as they felt it would give me better university options and therefore improve my career prospects. The sixth form facility I chose to study A levels at was the LaSwap Consortium in the borough of Camden.

For my A level subjects, I chose English, Sociology, History and Performing Arts. I felt my skills and passion were stronger in these subjects as opposed to Psychology, Mathematics and the

Sciences which were the suggested study subjects if one wanted to pursue a Psychology degree.

In 2007 I received B, A, A, B grades respectively for these subjects.

To become a qualified Educational Psychologist, a student was normally required to study Psychology at university or gain a postgraduate qualification in Psychology. Although, this was the advice given by the career services, I still felt better skilled and more passionate about studying Sociology at university level. Therefore, when it came to choosing subjects to study at university, I had decided to opt for Sociology related subjects, as opposed to pure Psychology. However, I was delighted when I came across one university for which I did not have to make a choice between Sociology and Psychology, as it provided the option to study these subjects together. This was the University of Cambridge.

I had first learnt about the University of Cambridge whilst studying at LaSwap and this is where I received the training to succeed with the application and interview processes that admission involved. So, thankfully, it seems that my secondary school teachers had been right to suggest that I study at this prestigious sixth form facility.

# *University of Cambridge*

Between 2007 and 2010, I completed my study of Social and Political Sciences at the University of Cambridge. This was a Bachelor of Arts degree and involved studying Psychology, Sociology, Social Anthropology and Politics in the first year, followed by papers in Sociology and Psychology in the second and third years.

Although I was ecstatic about being granted the privilege to study at the University of Cambridge, sadly it transpired to be, at most, unenjoyable experience for me. For the most part, I felt alone and unsupported. I think this was mainly due to the fact that I was one of only five black students out of a total of 500 students at Emmanuel College, most of whom were Caucasian. I felt that, because of my ethnicity, this very student body made assumptions far too easily about who I was and why I was at the University. It seemed that they avoided having meaningful conversation or interactions with me and, for the most part, avoided making eye contact with me. At times I felt invisible and constantly strived to try to fit in. Consequently, and unsurprisingly, I felt very alone and alienated.

When it came to my work, I did not feel that the environment was conducive for me to really fully explore concepts and have purposeful and meaningful discussions about the subject matter. Subsequently, I felt that this was reflected in my grades. On the morning of the 26th of June 2010, I received my final result from the University of Cambridge...it was a Third class degree.

# The Dismal Degree Result

Alone, I wept bitterly in my dorm room after receiving news of my degree result. My world had been shattered, my future blurred and my hopes of ever becoming a teacher catastrophically destroyed. What a disaster! I felt so embarrassed. I was not sure what to do next, how to rectify the situation. Head in hands, I bawled tears of sorrow for a very long time, until I really could cry no more.

For those not familiar with the English University grading system, a 3rd class degree is two levels above a fail, representing a result of around 40% out of 100%. Receiving a 3rd also meant that one was not automatically accepted for graduate schemes or for post graduate study, particularly a Post Graduate Certificate in Education (PGCE) which was the qualification I needed to become a teacher. Most institutions demand at least a 2:1 or 2:2 degree as the minimum requirement for entry onto a PGCE course.

Despite my 3rd class degree result, I still attempted to apply for entry onto PGCE courses. I felt that, as I had committed to three arduous years of study, I had earned a degree qualification, studied at one of the most prestigious universities in the world and learnt something of value, particularly from my Sociology of Education course, I should be considered as a candidate for a place on a PGCE course. However, regardless of my many application attempts, the answer was always the same – no, sorry we cannot accept a 3rd Class Degree, sorry a 3rd Class is too low. It was dismal. I had endured so much: the alienation, the humiliation, the lack of understanding, the feeling of being unable to make a significant contribution within my peer group, the indifference, the inability to reach my full potential and engage in meaningful discussions about my work.

I had nonetheless been able to push through, enduring those three years and graduating with a degree; not a pass, not a fail, but a degree, and the answer was still no. What did they want to me to do with the time I had invested? The knowledge that I had gained? Waste all the potential that was waiting to be untapped? Destroy the dream that I still wanted to achieve? At each no, I cried. At each no, I felt low.

***Consequently, here began my pit-stop at B.***

# Defining B

I will just take a moment here to briefly describe the bleakness of B. B: Not the desired profession or goal (e.g. teaching); not the future that one had envisioned. B is the mundane that you have accepted; the job that you have taken because it is a job and it pays the bills; the situation that you have accepted because you feel that it is what you deserve. Waking up in the morning without caring about something, devoid of a feeling of passion about anything and a total absence of the sense that today you will use your skills, gifts and qualities to make a difference and to create an impact.

No setting of meaningful goals; no setting of goals that will break you free from your comfort zone, the goals that keep you awake at night or wake you up early morning with ideas and enthusiasm and excitement. No ticking off when meaningful goals are reached. No joy at the end of the day, or week, or months. No looking back and smiling about what you have achieved.

No looking back and celebrating yourself and what you are and do. No overall vision or motivation that drives you. Simply dragging yourself through the day, mundanely carrying out commitments without excitement or purpose. Perhaps depression, perhaps a sense of dis-appointment with yourself. Perhaps suicidal thoughts.

If you recognise that you are now at B, please I would like you to stop and complete the section below.

## <u>Understanding your B</u>

*What would you say your B is?*
*Describe this position.*

# *Why do you feel like this is your B?*

## How do you feel about being in this position?

*Do you want to move on from this position? Why?*

# *More insight into my B: The banking job*

In view of the fact that I was not able to immediately enter into postgraduate study and pursue my career goal, I was advised by a friend to apply for any job at all in the interim. She worked for a bank and knew that they were currently recruiting.

I went along to the recruitment day and it transpired that the highest qualification required was a GCSE level C in Mathematics. Clearly, the bank was impressed with my CV and the level of qualifications I held and immediately offered me the role of Personal Banking Manager.

I began working for the bank in September 2010, 3 months after my graduation. To some extent, I was happy that I had a job in the city and had started at a secondary level position. However, I knew I was not completely passionate about working in this role or indeed within the banking and finance sector.

Although I performed the role to the best of my ability, cold calling clients to make appointments, selling loans and credit cards to customers, conducting customer interviews, providing information about accounts, every single day I had to motivate myself to go to work and some days even convince myself that I had to stay in the building at all.

I did not feel naturally skilled to perform the role, nor was I passionate about it. I did not feel I was working towards 'something', there was no "bigger picture" for me. Where, in this job, was I using my skills and knowledge from Social Sciences? Where, in this job, was I impacting positively upon people's lives? Where, in this job, was I listening to people's social or personal problems and providing advice to help them? I knew that I needed a change.

I endured the role for 8 months, until May 2011, when I handed in my resignation, leaving the job shortly afterwards. I truly believed that I was destined to achieve greater things and knew that I needed to start taking steps to make that a reality. After leaving my position at the bank, I took some time to think about my desired career choice and to research what actions I could take to help me to achieve this.

# My C

Again, let me remind you of what my C was. C represented beginning work as a qualified primary school teacher.

To some, this might sound like a simplistic goal. However, to me, this meant gaining a professional qualification, having a career, receiving a respectable graduate level of pay, earning regular income, doing something I was passionate about, doing something I felt as though I was gifted to do, having stability and financial security and pursuing further study. Finally, this would be the foundation upon which the rest of my life would be built. So, no, it was not just a simplistic goal.

So, now I want to ask you, what is your C? What are you really passionate about? What do you feel you are naturally gifted at or skilled to do?

What would you want to wake up and do every morning, without feeling that it was a bore or a chore? What would keep you driven? What excites you?

I would encourage you to take some time to identify that today. Take a few minutes now to fill in the section below:

## *Defining your C*

1. List three things that you are passionate about:

## 2. If money was not an issue, what path would your life follow? What would you do?

## 3. What is stopping you from currently doing this job/role/task?

4. List 5 key skills and gifts that you think you have. You could list a combination of both skills and gifts, or five key skills or five gifts.

*Skills are things that you do particularly well, which you might have had training for (e.g. sewing, speaking), whereas a gift is something you did not necessarily have training for but something that you do well naturally (e.g. singing, helping others, hairdressing).*

5. Which of these specific skills or gifts would you say would help you to do the desired job or role mentioned above (Question 2)?

6. What other job/career could these skills or gifts lead you to?

7. What could you do to take you closer to the
career/role of your choice? List 5 steps.

Ok. Let's talk now about how, after receiving a Third-class degree from Cambridge University and taking an unscheduled pit-stop at B, I nevertheless then went on to achieve my dream career.

## *After the banking job*

So, after I left the banking job, I knew that I would firstly need to gain some relevant experience working with children and young people. If not for the experience alone, this may also provide a route into a relevant and related career; e.g. working with young people, making a difference in their lives. So, I began to research jobs and work experience within the youth work and education sectors.

It was not long before I came across a youth charity based in Hackney. The charity, Off Centre, provided counselling, art therapy, mentoring and psychosocial activities for young people. With my background in Sociology and Psychology and my passion to make an impact upon the lives of children and young people, this was a perfect opportunity to gain experience and do something meaningful. I contacted the project leader of the psychosocial department and expressed my interest in volunteering at the charity. A few days later, I was called in for an interview.

Armed with evidence of my experience and qualifications, I attended the interview as a prospective volunteer but I was seeking more than just work experience, I wanted a job. Unbelievably, what I desired was exactly what transpired. The project leader offered me a short, paid internship working as a project assistant. I was completely ecstatic. I had a job where I would be doing something meaningful. However, I knew the satisfaction was only temporary, this was not a permanent position, nor was it a professional career position, and so obviously did not represent 'C'.

After my disastrous degree result, I was simply glad that I was now in the sector that I wanted to work in and was also able to use my skills to impact lives. Certainly, it was nowhere near the desired salary or career I wanted to ultimately achieve but I was happily on route to C. Although I enjoyed working at Off Centre, I knew that this would not provide a direct route to my desired career in teaching, however, I did not let this dream die.

With that goal very much in mind, I began to apply at postgraduate level again believing, this time, that the additional experience I had gained working at the Charity would be significant. I still had faith that I could be and should be successful, despite my degree classification. However, after another round of applications, I still failed to access the postgraduate study I desired. I was again disheartened. Would my dream die? Did the entire universe not think I was good enough?

Despite my personal, one to one conversations with Admission tutors, visits to universities, personal emails and approaches, experience, knowledge and my vision for my future, my third-class degree qualification was simply not good enough. That is all that I heard, again and again. What about me as a person? Why judge me based on a degree result? I was dispirited.

However, despite all of this, I did not let the desire to achieve my career goal die. I continued to believe in myself, my knowledge, my skills and my expectations for the future. So, while working at the Charity, I spoke to a friend who worked at a school, hoping that she might arrange some work experience for me there. I knew that this was a requirement of the PGCE course. I was so grateful to be offered two weeks of work experience at her school which would be the first time I had worked in a primary school.

After the two weeks of work experience had come to an end, I knew that I wanted to continue working at the school if possible. I asked the Headteacher if I could continue to work there on a voluntary basis for two days a week. I was delighted when she agreed to my request. So I worked three days at the Charity and the other two days at the school. As the school year came to an end in July 2012, I also chose to round up my volunteering experience then.

In contrast, a month later, in August 2012, my internship and time at the Charity abruptly ended; the funding for my specific role had ceased. I had spent 14 months working there, far longer than I had expected when I first started. I was terribly disillusioned. Since I had not been successful with the postgraduate applications, I had hoped that I could have continued to work permanently at the Charity, making a difference, perhaps carving out a career in the youth sector. However, this was not to be, and I now had to rely on my faith again to keep me on track to reach my goal. Still determined to pursue a career in teaching, I started to apply for teaching assistant roles. Although I honestly felt that I was overqualified for this position, I still applied, in the hope that it could be a possible route to C. While applying for teaching assistant positions, the Headteacher whose school I had volunteered at, contacted me to tell me there was a teaching assistant positon available at her school.

I was pleasantly surprised. I had been putting her down as a referee on my application forms but had not expected there to be an opening at her school. I went along for the interview, hoping to be successful and indeed, the same day, I was offered the job which I readily accepted. It was not the position I ultimately desired but there was no doubt that I was now getting a lot closer to C.

## *Working as a Teaching Assistant*

During the 19 months I spent working as a Teaching Assistant I was able to utilise my knowledge and skills as well as gaining experience. I used my time there to observe the teachers as well as to enquire about their role; asking questions such as what did they enjoy about being a teacher, was there any part of the role they did not enjoy? I remained convinced that this was the career that I wanted to pursue. I made this known to the staff there, as well as to the Headteacher, hoping that I would gain support with entry into teacher training. Frustratingly however, my degree classification was still an issue. I failed to reach my desired career through this route as well so, again, I had to take matters into my own hands.

# *Applying for Postgraduate study – again*

Still determined that I had the skills and knowledge to work as a teacher, I continued to research and enquire about teacher training. I discovered a training scheme called School Direct, where individuals could train directly with a school and receive a teaching qualification. I was convinced that this was the route for me. As I continued to research, I came across an institution that provided School Direct training, specifically for schools in East London. This institution was called SCITTELS. Having grown up in Hackney, I was even more persuaded that this was the route for me. Additionally, this route also provided a PGCE qualification which meant that I would not just receive National Qualified Teacher (NQT) status, but would receive a postgraduate qualification as well. This was important to me, I wanted to learn about the theory of education and teaching, as well as engage with the practical side.

Only too aware of my unsuccessful track record with PGCE applications, I contacted the recruitment tutor at SCITTELS personally to explain my situation and she was very positive, advising me to apply. I was a little more hopeful, although this would be the third year spent applying for teacher training.

It was not long before I heard back from SCITTELS. To my shock, they offered me a conditional place on their programme of study. Of all the many applications I had made, this was the first time I had been successful! I was, at last, extremely hopeful.

## *Interview time*

Although I had been conditionally offered a place, I was still very nervous about the interview process. This would be my one opportunity to secure the place. As I waited in the interview room, I felt very apprehensive, I did not know what to expect. I was one of four candidates waiting to hear further instructions and when the process was explained to us, I was quietly confidently but still very nervous. I was anxious because I felt that this was my one and only chance to be successful. Throughout my journey from A to C, I had never had such a good opportunity.

During the interview process, we were required to teach a mini lesson. I cannot quite remember what I taught but I did feel that my lesson was successful, more so because I remember being able to smile after the teaching session ended. When it came to the interview process, again I was fairly confident. Not only did I feel that I was armed with the skills, experience and qualities needed to be a teacher, I was bolstered by the fact that I had been offered an interview, a stage in the process that I had not reached before.

I felt that I was able to answer all of the questions, so I felt very confident about my ability to be successful at the end of the interview process. Interestingly, the interviewer highlighted the fact that I repeatedly mentioned my failure at Cambridge University during the interview and asked me to expand on my reason for doing so. I explained that I believed that previous postgraduate organisations had not accepted me on their programmes due to my degree result, but I did not, however, feel that the degree result was a reflection of my true ability. I highlighted my vision of making a difference to and impacting upon the lives of young people, as a teacher, as well as the skills and experience I had gained since my graduation. Noticeably, I received positive body signals from the interviewer and I was very hopeful.

I cannot quite remember how long I had to wait to hear back from the institution, but I do not think it was more than a week. Nor can I quite remember if I received the news via a phone call or by email. However, I do remember that when I received the news that I had been successful at the interview process and had been offered a place on the School Direct programme, I was in awe and utter shock, left completely speechless. My exact thoughts were: Me? After all those attempts? The door had finally opened. I could have cried that day. Actually, I believe I did. I phoned my mum and family to tell them the good news and they were all so happy for me!

Finally, my opportunity had arrived. I was standing at the door to my teaching training programme and was about to enter. My time at 'B' was about to come to an end. I was due to start training in September 2014, so, humbly and thankfully, I left the teaching assistant job in July.

# Training as a teacher

I started teacher training in September 2014 and felt more than ready to take on the task. Although it meant that I had to leave the teaching assistant post, I was not too disappointed. I was now approaching C.

Upon starting the course, the expectations and workloads were laid out exceptionally well. We had to submit two written assignments which included a research project, complete a task file for each term and take on the responsibility of teaching 80% of the lessons for primary school pupils which typically consisted of Mathematics, English, Science, Geography, History, Physical Education, Religious Education, a language (e.g. French or Spanish) and Music. Certainly, it was very challenging. I had many late nights, tears, pressure, embarrassment, fear, unsuccessful lesson observations and teaching sessions but, despite all of that, I knew that I wanted to qualify and work as teacher. I kept going. I kept my belief alive.

## *Applying for jobs*

In the early days of our training we were advised to apply for jobs for the following school year beginning in September. I applied to two Newly Qualified Teacher (NQT) teaching pools and was successfully accepted. Although, I was offered a job at one school via one of the NQT pools, I had my hopes set on working at a particular school which I felt was ideal for me, focusing as it did on the creative arts. So, unfortunately, I decided to decline the offer and to contact the other school directly. After attending an interview there, I was offered a position at the school beginning in September 2015.

I was simply ecstatic and accepted the offer straight away. All I needed to do now was successfully complete my training. Naturally, there was a fear that, just like my Cambridge degree, I could fail. However, I did acknowledge that I felt more able to be myself in this environment, I felt more recognised and valued and I felt I had prior deeper subject knowledge and experience and was therefore better equipped to succeed.

## *Completing the training*

After 11 months of hard work and determination, in July 2015 I successfully completed my PGCE training. What was my emotion? Utter joy. That goal that I had set myself so long ago, I had finally achieved. After five long years, thankfully, all my efforts and endeavors had not been in vain.

## *Summary*

Seven years earlier, my whole world had been thrown into darkness. I was both embarrassed and shocked by the degree result that I had been awarded. I was not sure how I could rectify this step and get myself back on track. Although I had taken so many steps to try to reach my destination - resigning from a stable job, working at a youth charity, volunteering at a primary school, working as a Teaching Assistant, constantly applying for postgraduate teacher training places - I faced a lot of rejection along the way and, consequently, it seemed that I would never reach the end of my journey and arrive at my desired destination.

Upon reflection, I was grateful that I had a good enough foundation from where I began, all that time ago at A, to set me on the right course towards my goal. I was raised in a secure, loving household, had access to education and excellent teachers and had attended good schools. I had a passion for learning and was focused and dedicated. Importantly, I had a vision for where I wanted to go in life: a career goal.

Your 'A' might not look the same as mine, the beginning of your journey may be very different. However, what is important is that you set yourself a goal, this could be a career goal, a financial or personal goal, your own C. There will no doubt be something within you that will help to drive you towards your C.

Identify what you are passionate about, the gifts and skills that you have and how you want to impact and influence the world. If you have not done so already, use the section on page 31, Defining your C, to help you to do this.

Now that you have completed 'Defining your C', please take the time to complete 'Achieving at your C' below:

# Achieving your C

## My career/life goal is: (E.g. Teacher)

# When do I want to achieve my career goal by? (e.g. July 20--)

# What steps do I need to take to achieve my career goal ?

| STEPS /GOALS | HOW? | WHEN? |
| --- | --- | --- |
| E.g. Gain teaching experience (work at least 2 weeks in a school) | Contact local schools asking for experience; hand in CV to school | By the end 17th February 20-- |
|  |  |  |
|  |  |  |
|  |  |  |

# What stumbling blocks are currently in my way?

# Why do I see this as a stumbling block?

# What could I do to help me overcome this/these stumbling blocks?

| WHAT | HOW | WHEN |
| --- | --- | --- |
| E.g. Retrain (repeat my degree) | Apply to UCAS again | By December 20-- |
| Gain more experience | Contacting specific schools | By May 20-- |
| | | |
| | | |
| | | |

58

How will I feel once I have achieved this career goal?

Remember, obstacles may appear on your journey to C, they did for me. These obstacles may well be unexpected and unplanned, for example like my degree result was for me. What is important is that you take time to acknowledge, understand and learn from any setback. If you do not acknowledge it, it can be used as an excuse to remain at B.

When I got my degree result, it led me to ask a range of questions: why did I end up getting this result? What did I do that contributed to this? Did I not have enough background knowledge or was it that I did not receive enough support while I was there? Or was it simply not the right type of learning environment for me?

I felt that by asking myself these questions I would empower myself to move forward and act. I really had to accept the answers that followed from them. I concluded that I had done the best that I could when I was at university and that all my knowledge, skills and experience were not in vain. I did not believe that a simple setback should stop me from achieving my dreams. I had to find an alternative route to C.

Only when I did this, did I find the courage and the energy to reroute to C.

When your obstacles and setbacks arise, you will most likely have to find an alternative route to your C. Take time out to reflect and research and then act.

Get up from B, gather your resources, pack your bags and make a start towards C, always with the belief that you will arrive!

It might not be a smooth journey to C, as you saw from my experience. I received a lot of knocks along the way, but I kept pushing, I kept kicking, I kept believing in myself, I kept walking. Someone saw my potential, recognised my knowledge, my passion, my skills. They believed in my vision, just as I did, and they opened the door for me. They provided that opportunity for me.

This is a lesson for you. People are your helpers; a person is the doorway to your next opportunity. Connect with others, be ready to network, think about how you present yourself as you leave home, on social media, while you talk on the phone, on the internet. Does everything you do point towards your destiny? Do you communicate as a potential teacher, lawyer or whatever destination you have defined as your C? Do you communicate your passion when you meet with others?

In conclusion, think about how you act, what you say, does it communicate to others where you want to go (C), or does it say to them I am content at B?

If you are at A, map out your journey.

If you are at B, acknowledge your setback, learn from it, empower yourself, research and take action. Most importantly, do not choose to stay at B. **KEEP WALKING!**

If you are on route to C, congratulations. **KEEP WALKING!**

If you are at your C, congratulations for arriving! Now I want to encourage you to pursue more goals and start new journeys! Your greater self awaits!

Keep Walking!

***Thank you for reading!***
***Mavela.***

# *Author Information*

Mavela Owusu Boahen, lives in London, England, with her husband, Daniel (Joe), and one year old son Kweku Sebastian.

Although she works full-time as a qualified Primary school Teacher, she is very active within the women's and children's ministry at her church, taking on roles such the Secretary and Vice President. She is also part of the church choir.

Mavela's hobbies include: singing, dancing and reading.

Mavela has thoroughly enjoyed writing her first book and hopes to write a range of other books in the future.

www.ingramcontent.com/pod-product-compliance
Lightning Source LLC
Chambersburg PA
CBHW061434050726
47593CB00006B/2342